TV Coverage of the Oil Crises:
How Well Was the Public Served?

Volume III
An Economist's Perspective
1973-74/1978-79

A Commentary by
Thomas W. Hazlett

(the media institute)

First printing September 1982.

Published by The Media Institute, Washington, D.C.

Printed in the United States of America.

ISBN: 0–937790–08–7

Library of Congress Catalog Card Number: 81–86030

Table of Contents

Foreword

As the earlier volumes of this study concluded, TV network news was deficient in several major ways in its coverage of the oil crises of 1973–74 and 1978–79. The networks' infatuation with non-market solutions such as regulation and price controls, their preference for government sources and concomitant lack of interest in outside experts, and their wholesale neglect of the crises' economic and historical dimensions were just a few indications that something had gone awry in TV news coverage.

Volumes I and II brought to light these and other aspects of network news coverage in a massive research effort involving 1,462 oil stories. But it remains for this third and final volume, a commentary by Thomas W. Hazlett, professor of economics at California State University at Fullerton, to place these research findings in greater perspective.

We asked Mr. Hazlett to examine the findings of Volumes I and II in comparing the networks' presentation of the crises with the economic realities of those shortages. Mr. Hazlett has responded by pointing out the wide and often yawning gap between the two; the reader will also benefit from his insightful analysis of the events and economic issues surrounding the oil crises.

While Mr. Hazlett's commentary should not necessarily be regarded as a reflection of The Media Institute's views, we feel its inclusion adds a perspective (the kind of informed perspective so often lacking in TV news coverage) which will enhance the reader's appreciation of Volumes I and II and lead to a greater understanding of TV's performance in covering this major economic story.

Leonard J. Theberge
President
The Media Institute

Network coverage failed to give the viewing public sufficient information to make an informed judgment about the oil crises.

Volume I
TV Coverage of
the Oil Crises:
How Well Was
the Public Served?

Introduction

With only the treacherous exceptions of political assassination and international terrorism, no single issue has so shaken America's balance in this turbulent epoch than the amalgam of super-events clumped together in the household headline: "Oil Crisis." This nation's collective ego has never, perhaps, suffered anything like the triple flurry of Vietnam-Watergate-Oil Crisis, yet it is the latter—a purely *economic* problem—to which America was allegedly most immune. And as an economic crisis, the oil dilemma spilled throughout society. Whereas Vietnam enveloped the men who fought there and the campuses that protested going, and Watergate was, for most people, a crisis-by-Evening News, not a line of newspaper print was necessary to unmask the oil crisis; most Americans were in it before they read about it.

The oil crisis (or more precisely the two separate crises of 1973–74 and 1978–79) dramatically reshaped our foreign policy, particularly our view of the Third World. It touched every side of our domestic

The author wishes to thank Professor Edward W. Erickson of North Carolina State University for a conscientious critique of a previous draft of this paper.

economy from, as Ronald Reagan puts it, "Wall Street to Main Street." It hurled colossal issues into the public arena, and even inspired a whole new metaphysic for the decade in which it struck. The American experience of the 1970s was profoundly styled by the two words "oil crisis."

What the nation's most important news medium, television network evening news, said about this mega-crisis is the subject of this study. Our research overlaps the two periods of U.S. *retail* gas shortages: October 1973—May 1974 and November 1978—August 1979. All three network evening news broadcasts were surveyed during this period using a process known as content analysis. Researchers at The Media Institute in Washington, D.C., utilizing television tapes from archives at Vanderbilt University, reviewed a total of 1,462 separate news stories lasting 39½ hours. The statistical findings of The Media Institute, which have been published as Volumes I and II of this study, provide data on television's performance in covering the crisis. Comparing the networks' performance with the actual economics of the crises is the purpose of this final volume.

The networks demonstrated an overreliance on government sources for information about the causes of and solutions to the oil crises.

Volume I

Chapter I

Perhaps the complexity of the oil crises was too great for any of us to expect they would be adequately explained by the television news medium. Perhaps the issues went well beyond the scope of 90-second film clips. Perhaps the market for rock-bottom explanations just wasn't to be found amongst viewers who were prepared to witness nothing more challenging than a reporter interviewing a disgruntled motorist in a gasoline line.

Then again, perhaps the viewer deserved to know what was going on, and to hear it from news reporters who understood it themselves. Yet, as the data observed in this study starkly indicate, there was virtually no causal link between the political economy of the oil crises and the television news reportage of those crises. Opting to broadcast personalized dramas of emotive value, and essentially to side-step any dalliance with dispassionate analysis, televised news may simply have been bowing to the confines of its market. Still, it is disappointing that such a blanket black-out on the actual economic forces at work could infect and debilitate the coverage of assuredly capable newscasters.

The most striking aspect of the news was the raw

fact that 56% of the sources utilized by the television networks were on the government payroll. (In stories discussing solutions to the crises, government sources were used 77% of the time.) In contrast, only 2% of all sources were of the outside "expert" category. From where was the news to get its "analysis"? (The oil companies were the second most frequent source (17%) and it is clear that most oil executives had their own hidden agendas to advance—like the perpetuation of favorable and unreported regulatory schemes). It can hardly be argued that the oil crises were less far-reaching in their consequences than the Watergate episode, but we can at least be confident that in the latter the news media did not content themselves by simply taking the government's word.

We are not surprised to find that government sources talk of government solutions, and infrequently of government botches. In a regulatory regime fraught with counterproductive policy measures and loopholes awarding billions to warring partisans, it appears incredible with hindsight (and statistical fact) that the news establishment did not frantically run to embrace outside experts to help them chart the way. "News executives should once and for all abandon the notion," declares Hodding Carter in a recent *Newsweek*, "that generalists weaned on political reporting can adequately cover the many revolutions under way at home and abroad.... Far more reporters should be assigned to the still all but unexplored ghettos—not simply of race and class, but of economics, science, academic research and religious revival."[1] Nowhere is this verity more glaring than in the inability of TV news to separate fact from fantasy in the oil debate.

News reporters are, after all, generalists. This is by design, and it has its value. Yet news by non-experts

---

[1]Hodding Carter, "The Myopic Press," in My Turn Column, *Newsweek* Magazine, December 7, 1981.

requires a devotion to research and inquiry that is easily deferred. The problem with going to the "involved" parties for the story, of course, is that it is hard to *learn* the economics of the situation. What came out of this style was precisely what one would expect from such a situation: news reporters were "covering" events before they figured out the story; the result was that the story *never* made it to the camera.

Having little idea of what lay at the bottom of "shortages", gas lines, high prices and the rest, news reporters fell into the mode of following around frustrated and antagonistic parties with microphones. These actors engaged in conflicts which were often multi-sided, as the government, opposition political leaders, "Big Oil", OPEC, American consumers, environmentalists, service station operators and other crises "participants" clashed against one another in varied team groupings. But how it all came out for the television news audience was a matter of drama, not of analysis, because the medium itself had no idea of the dynamics of the problem or, therefore, of the *economic interests* of the groups that clashed.

What we must focus on in analyzing the value of reporting content, then, is this "big picture:" first, did the reporting *methods* make sense in uncovering the dimensions of the problem, and second, did the medium fundamentally grasp the nature of what it reported upon? If our news sources performed well on these counts, we should be generously forgiving on missed forecasts concerning the pump price of unleaded. We suspect they will do better next time. But if the basic methods and analyses were wide of the mark, then even the boast of a bull's eye prediction regarding some specific statistic will do little to gain our confidence.

Sadly, as this examination for The Media Institute demonstrates, it is just on the principal counts of method and understanding that the breakdown of network television coverage of the oil crises is most apparent. The methodology of news gathering revealed in the statistics herein gives substance to the story of how one of the network Big Three chose its energy assignment reporters. Having assembled the company's elite journalistic corps, about 35 in number, at the New York headquarters in the early days of the 1973 embargo, the senior reporter asked: "How many gallons are in a barrel of oil?" The fortunate newsmen who answered "30" and "50" won themselves a new beat; they had narrowed in most closely on the correct reply of "42."

It became nearly impossible, then, for discussion to take place within a medium which had such a casual acquaintance with even the most basic facts of the issue. Americans were treated to oil crisis news as though we had no economic history, as if oil were the only scarce, finite resource that had ever graced the planet, or that America was the one and only country that was dealing with an oil crisis. With so little wordly experience to lean on, no wonder many Americans felt helplessly adrift in a vast and lonely sea of energy questions.

Fortunately, the oil crises of the past decade are handy problems to autopsy. One wonders if they were, in fact, created by a professor of literature, so neatly are their forms fitted to the pattern of beginning-middle-end. The oil crises, it will be explained below, were "policy induced"[2], and the *removal* of U.S. energy policy (most notably price controls on crude and refined petroleum products), has allowed the post-crises era to commence. And now we indulge the privilege of looking back to when we were "in it."

* * *

[2]E. W. Erickson and R. M. Spann, "The U.S. Petroleum Industry," in *The Energy Question, An International Failure of Policy*, E. W. Erickson and L. Waverman, editors (Toronto: University of Toronto Press, 1974), vol. 2, p. 7.

The market for energy will forever be the saving grace of textbook writers of economic theory. Even for this strange and plodding bunch, what could make an easier story? Allow two prominent textbook authors, Douglass North and Roger Leroy Miller, to clarify it by allowing you the opportunity to fill in the blanks in the following quotation:

> "The question concerning the duration of our present cheap supplies of _____ cannot but excite deep interest and anxiety.... The constant tendency of discovery is to render _____ a more and more efficient agent, while there is no probability that when our _____ is used up any more powerful substitute will be forthcoming.... We cannot make up for a future want of _____ by importation from other countries.... Considering how greatly our (industrial capacity) depends upon _____ and how vast is our consumption of it compared with that of other nations, it cannot be supposed that we shall do without it.... It is then simply inferred that we cannot long continue our present rate of progress."[3]

What have you deduced as the mystery noun? The presumption, of course, is *petrol,* and the date of this message must certainly fall in our very recent history ... perhaps in the mid to late 1970s, no?

No. If you scratch "oil" in favor of "coal," you will have an exact replica of a passage from William Stanley Jevon's *The Coal Question.* Copyright 1865. "In 1865 this famous economist was saying exactly the same things about coal that people are saying about oil today," observe North and Miller. "He was an expert and he was proven wrong: recoverable reserves of coal are estimated to be equivalent to 12 *trillion* barrels of

[3]Douglass C. North and Roger LeRoy Miller, *The Economics of Public Issues,* (New York: Harper and Row, 1980), pp. 3–5.

oil today. To understand why Jevon's prediction did not come true is to understand the roots of our current energy problems. . . ."[4]

The essential energy problem, now, then and forever, is clear: What will energy cost? We are no more "running out of energy" than we are running out of earth. The first consideration is the eminently obvious: energy is neither created nor destroyed, but simply transferred from one form to another. It is the *cost* of this transformation that concerns us—not the finite supply which shall forever remain fixed. Secondly, and most significantly, no indicative trends of supply and demand are to be taken seriously absent the equilibrating variable of *price*. Market forces will spontaneously be balanced by a price that fluctuates to the point where supply and demand are equivalent. A shortage will be ameliorated by a rise in price, which will expand supply *and* reduce demand. A surplus can be eliminated by a fall in price, for precisely the same factors in reverse. For these reasons, both surpluses and shortages are never "physical" or "technical" conditions of nature in some abstract sense—but "economic" problems stemming from a disruption of the natural price mechanism. In his epic *Knowledge and Decisions*, economist Thomas Sowell explains:

> All "shortages" and "surpluses" are *at some given price,* and not absolutely in terms of the scarcity or abundance of the item in qualitative terms. The severe housing shortage during World War II occurred with no significant change in either the amount of housing in the country or in the size of the population. Indeed, more than ten million people left the civilian population, and many left the country, during World War II. More housing was demanded by the remaining civilian population *at*

---

[4]IBID.

rent-controlled prices. The effective knowledge conveyed by artificially low prices was of far more abundant housing than actually existed or had ever existed.[5]

Being an economic problem, the shortage of housing, or energy, or any other commodity, involves specifically a failure of communication: While consumers would be *willing* to pay more for a given resource, say energy, the providers of such are not permitted to *hear* this demand, due to the transmission trouble called "price controls." At the very same time consumers are anxious for more energy, investors are building condos, or racetracks, or taking European vacations. Unless confronted by higher *prices* for the production of energy, these millions of potential suppliers won't even *know* what demands are going unsatisfied. This is, in all respects, a *coordination* problem. We fail to give the interlocking elements of the economic machine the chance to voice their demands and capabilities effectively across legal barriers.

Many people do not like competitive market prices. People in the oil business have traditionally disliked competitive prices for petroleum. Not surprisingly, they have considered them too *low.* For decades, as testimony to something politely identified as "political persuasiveness," the federal government agreed—and instituted policies bluntly designed to raise them. "Since at least the 1930s," writes Professor Clayburn LaForce, "the United States' petroleum market has been manipulated for political purposes. Regulation of crude began during the Great Depression, as state regulatory commissions estimated the demand for crude and used this estimate to regulate the output of every well. In the late 1950s the federal government added restrictions on imports of foreign crude, the

---

[5]Thomas Sowell, *Knowledge and Decisions* (New York: Basic Books, 1980), pp. 176–177.

objective of these 'quotas' being higher prices for domestic producers. They were successful. In addition to higher prices for crude, we got an energy lobby and a lot of richer oilmen."[6] The import controls alone are estimated to have cost the general public about $5 billion annually, measured in 1969 dollars (or roughly $14 billion in 1982 dollars).[7] Of this surcharge on oil, about half went into the pockets of oil investors and half went straight down the drain—what the economists call "dead-weight losses."

In the years prior to the 1970s, federal policy was a little paradoxical—but only a little. That is, countervailing policies were effected which served to lower oil prices, and hence *encourage* consumption, in the form of tax breaks for oil depletion and "intangible" drilling cost write-offs. These caused the profitability of oil drilling to increase, thereby drawing in additional investment capital, expanding the available supply, and thus lowering the market price of refined oil at the pump. Yet these price depressants, which also had the unfortunate side-effect of dissipating America's crude reserves in the pre-OPEC days, were generally dwarfed by the price-enhancing forces of the import quotas. President Eisenhower adopted such controls against imports in the popular name of "national security," prompting the well-known economist George Stigler to refer sheepishly to the great horse-laughs this argument must have evoked at the Petroleum Club.[8] "Such laughter aside," wrote Stigler, "if national defense were the goal of the quotas, a tariff would be a more economical instrument of policy: it

---

[6] J. Clayburn LaForce, "The Energy Crisis: The Moral Equivalent of Bamboozle," Original Paper No. 11 by the International Institute for Economic Research, April 1978, p. 9.

[7] IBID., p. 10.

[8] George Stigler, "The Theory of Economic Regulation," in the *Bell Journal of Economics and Management Science*, (Spring 1971), and reprinted in Stigler, *The Citizen and the State: Essays on Regulation* (Chicago: The University of Chicago Press, 1975), p. 115.

would retain the profits of exclusion for the Treasury." The logic of limiting exports to prepare for war is (was) equally shaky. British journalist Norman Macrae makes just the opposite national security case: "In preparation for the day when foreign oil supplies become unreliable, it was then desirable to keep as much American oil in the ground as possible."[9]

The common thread running throughout these partially offsetting policies is translucent: they all had the unambiguous effect of raising oil company profits. And, on net, they raised oil product prices as well. Then in one sweeping stroke, with President Nixon's economy-wide price controls announced on August 15, 1971, the United States Government launched a ten-year battle to *suppress* the price of oil *below* its market level. The success of this policy is easily tested. In 1970 "uncontrolled" (i.e., where price controls were set too high to make any difference) gasoline, sold for whatever the oil giants wanted to charge (and the market would bear), and cost 35.69¢ a gallon. In 1980, after a decade of "protection from price gouging," "controlled" gasoline was available for $1.24 a gallon.[10] Why did the controls fail to attain their stated objective?

Imposed at a time when we were, in fact, running out of "cheap" oil, the controls started a ten-year decline in U.S. oil drilling and production by freezing prices such that oil production became less profitable. This was not decided by a secret petroleum consortium—but by an inevitable social process. That is, there are any number of possible places for capitalists to invest their dollars. If the oil price control lowers

---

[9]Norman Macrae, "British Media and Energy Policy," paper presented at the International Conference on Media Coverage of the Energy Crisis, Ditchley Park, England, October 23–25, 1981, p. 2.

[10]Platt's Oilgram Price Service and the United States Department of Energy, as reprinted in "United States Petroleum Statistics: 1981 Revised" (Washington, D.C.: Independent Petroleum Association of America, 1981).

the returns to be gained from oil drilling, this is precisely analogous to saying that the cost of all *alternative* investments, say in wine-growing, or motion picture producing, or fried chicken franchising, have become lessened. Investments are not made abstractly, by committees that "know" what will most enhance consumer welfare. In point of fact, it is through the price system, and the quest to make profits and avoid losses, that investors are *shown* what the consumers most desire to have made available, given the cost of providing it. (This cost, it should be noted, is what the supplier must pay to outbid competing consumers for all the resources required to produce the good and, hence, represents a close measure of the value of the opportunities sacrificed by making the product in question.) The most profitable opportunities are those where the prices buyers are willing to *pay* are the greatest when compared to the opportunity *cost* of selling that product to them. When lower prices for suppliers were signalled, the discovery and production of price-controlled oil was curtailed.

But while price controls could, and did, discourage American investors from investing risk capital to bring oil to market, these controls could not discourage consumers from filling up at the pump. As a matter of fact, they did just the reverse: low prices sweetened the lure of the gas station pit stop. The year 1972 was a record one for gas consumption and 1973 topped that. U.S. oil production, which peaked in 1970, declined in these years. The difference was filled in the international market.

The now famous October 1973 Arab oil boycott was noteworthy to its American audience in at least two respects: (1) it brought the dilemma to a boil, delivering the simmering shortage right to your local gas station; (2) it was the *second* time the Arabs had collectively embargoed the United States, and no one even remembered the first. "In 1967, during the Six-

Day War," notes a recent volume on the oil shortage, "every Arab producer except Algeria had totally shut down its oil fields. But the United States, Venezuela, and Indonesia had responded by increasing production. Within a few weeks the embargo was a shambles."[11]

What had changed between 1967 and 1973 was primarily a domestic matter: U.S. price controls. In the late 1960s the U.S. oil industry, responding to price incentives, was expanding. In the early 1970s the U.S. oil industry, again responding to price incentives, was *contracting*. While crude oil imports increased less than 18% between 1962 and 1970, they virtually *doubled* in just the first two years of domestic price controls, 1971–1973.[12] Imports of all petroleum products jumped 37%.[13] America was caught leaning on foreign oil and OPEC cashed in.

Revealingly, the American gasoline shortage *predated* the Arab oil embargo by several months. It was not in October 1973 that motorists first began their service station queues—but the previous April and May. The reason was clear: President Nixon had reimposed price controls on petroleum products in March 1973 (all other sectors were being decontrolled in Phase III of Nixon's New Economic Policy) because the Administration saw tight energy markets pushing the price of oil higher. Rather than allowing the self-correcting price mechanism to bring forth the necessary adjustments (increasing conservation and production), the Administration clamped on controls just as prices were going up—and Americans were soon parked in gas lines. Importantly (and ominously), the shortage was temporarily alleviated only by allowing

---

[11]H. A. Merklein and William P. Murchison, *Those Gasoline Lines and How They Got There* (Dallas: The Fisher Institute, 1980), p. 21.

[12]U.S. Department of Energy, reprinted in "Petroleum Statistics ... ", supra. note 10.

[13]IBID.

U.S. refiners to pull greater oil supplies from foreign sources.

"The increase in gasoline supplies, according to Richard H. Leet, vice-president for supply and distribution at Amoco Oil Co., is a direct result of an increase in imported oil and higher utilization of U.S. refineries," noted *Business Week* on July 7, 1973 when the Spring crisis had abated. "Scrapping import tickets and replacing them with the more straightforward import duties, he contends, allows oil companies to buy more and plan better, which adds up to more gasoline for the consumer." And more reliance on OPEC.

This was, of course, a dress rehearsal for the full-blown crisis of six months hence. It is revealing that television news skipped past this harbinger with an astonishingly blank stare; a tiny percentage of all stories on the Arab oil embargo noted that the shortage came prior to the embargo. The lessons of the first 1973 gas shortage were manifest: OPEC was not the root cause, binding price controls mean gas lines, domestic crude oil shortages are plugged by the foreign oil market. Yet these lessons were neither digested nor reported by network television news.

The networks gave scant attention to the issues on which many economists and experts believe the crises hinged. Instead, television entertained at great length a popular notion that the crises were the fault of, and perhaps a hoax perpetrated by, the oil industry.

Volume I

Chapter II

OPEC was blessed by American ignorance. For OPEC's mission was never simple and it could not be accomplished without help. The key to any market restriction is to devise a mechanism for keeping out that ever-lurking evil, competition. When the monopolist, or cartel, cuts output to raise the ante, will there arise a new source of supply to abscond with their customers—and profits? OPEC faced just such a question, with an affirmative answer, in 1967.

By 1973, however, the U.S. Cost of Living Council was there to protect them. When OPEC cut back, U.S. domestic price controls on crude oil denied "windfall profits" to American producers. They saved the profits instead for OPEC. The domestic controls served to curtail the output of the largest free world producer of oil far more efficiently than OPEC could have ever hoped to do with agents of its cartel—and the enforcement of this cartel restriction of (U.S.) supply was handled by employees of the U.S. Government, paid by the U.S. taxpayer!

Did the American consumer benefit from this? Well ... that is a little embarrassing to explain. Prices at the well-head (crude oil) are a little different than prices at the pump (refined oil), or maybe a *lot* different. Crude oil could be kept at, controlled to, a price of zero, but this would hardly reduce the price at the pump. What the price control at the crude level does is to create a smaller supply of oil which, when refined, will consequently fetch a *higher* retail price (as consumers scramble to outbid each other for the scarcer commodity). This is just what happened with the oil price controls in the United States, with two exceptions: the crises of 1973–74 and 1978–79. These were the only two instances where the government controls pushed the price at the pump down under *its* market price; these were, as it turned out, the two times we waited in gasoline lines.

The shortages were, despite the media confusion and popular opinion ("seven in ten Americans thought the gasoline shortages were deliberately contrived by the oil companies"[14]), *prima facie* evidence that the oil companies were *not* in control. A gasoline line is proof that the consumer was willing to pay *above* the nominal price, as demonstrated by the fact that he was willing to pay *and* wait. The profit-maximizing course for the gas station, of course, is not to impose senseless burdens—like a two-hour wait—on customers, but to take their money. They would have gladly raised prices, and kept raising prices, until the shortage went to zero (i.e. the market "cleared"). The end of each crisis, we plainly saw, obtained just as soon as prices were raised to that point where the market-clearing level was reached. High prices, it should be remembered, are in the interests of oil owners and sellers; long lines are simply "dead-weight losses," what one economist at the time labeled the moral equivalent of "breaking crystal."

The manner in which television news stories presented the always attendant laws of supply and

---

[14]Adam Smith, *Paper Money*, (New York: Summit Books, 1981), p. 212.

demand illuminates the medium's revealed preference for *investigative* journalism over *analytical* journalism. Whenever just a glimpse of these forces was spotted (and always it was a glimpse, for a panoramic view of the entire situation would have ruined the story line) it seemed that the scene was used as backdrop for some expose of Sinister Forces. Take a lengthy report by NBC's Richard Hunt on March 13, 1974. He explains a complex tale concerning oil shipments from Turkey and Rumania. The problem addressed in the report is that no one can tell where the oil is actually coming from—it may, in fact, have originated in Saudi Arabia. The intimation is that, as a statement attributed to George Meany just before the Hunt story had suggested, "the oil shortage may have been at least partly contrived." After interviewing an American gasoline wholesaler and a service station operator in a vain attempt to find out whose oil we were buying, Hunt concludes, standing beside a Tarrytown, New York gas station: "The gasoline in this pump no doubt travelled a long way and passed through many hands to get here. Apparently every transaction was legal.... It seems to show that more gas is available, if people are willing to pay. Richard Hunt, NBC News, Tarrytown, New York."

This story was nearly identical (excepting names and places) to a report filed five years later by CBS correspondent John Sheehan. After tracking down a number of "middlemen" who were involved in arranging wholesale gasoline deliveries, an apparently surprised Sheehan watches a "consumer watchdog" from the American Automobile Association place an undercover call to an oil broker. "What we learned," the AAA official tells Sheehan, "is that there is fuel available for the price. There is fuel available."

On March 6, 1979 NBC's Jim Scott asked Pittsburgh gas station operator Micky Curtin what was making him so angry at his company. "I think there's a lot of gas out there, but I think they just want to get the prices up," Curtin said. "I think once the prices are up, there will be all the gas we can handle."

Television news demonstrated an uncanny knack in bringing out the issue in crystal clarity, i.e. higher prices will alleviate shortages—and then burying this essential truth beneath an avalanche of gut-level accusations as to *motives,* as if evil oil interests had themselves conspired to first invent and then impose the discipline of economic scarcity. With the shortage created by price controls staring them right in the face, they failed to take the hint; a mere 18% of the discussion concerning the causes of the crises even looked in the government's direction. According to Media Institute figures, a great number of these stories portrayed the problem as emanating from regulations that were too *lax.*

This journey right past the simple fact led to a widespread pre-occupation (in both crises) with the question, "is the crisis real?" The alternative to a "real crisis" was, of course, a manipulation of the consuming public by "Big Oil." The lure of this scenario was irresistable. Imagine asking yourself, Do you trust your Giant Oil Corporation? One finds oneself spitting at the very notion, particularly when still smarting from some very bad times in those foul gasoline queues. The market for 'Have You Hugged Your Seven Sisters Today?' bumperstickers appears rather thin. As John Chancellor informed his audience on March 19, 1979: "despite torrents of information, a lot of people still wonder if the shortages are real, or part of a scheme to make more money for the oil companies."

The television cameras seemed to run wherever a story exposing the necessity of paying a market-clearing price to get oil could be had. And the villian was clear—anyone who attempted to *charge* the market clearing price was causing the problem. This mode of analysis ended up with the story exactly backwards: middlemen and stations which were attempting to bring forth new supplies (by themselves paying higher prices in wholesale markets) were the culprits. Government officials, who were attempting to push prices back down to shortage-inducing levels, were portrayed as the *heroes*. This irony was stretched to incredulous limits when Walter Cronkite, on January 21, 1974 concluded a segment on "a hearing to determine whether there is a fuel shortage," by giving President Richard Nixon some badly needed positive publicity: "President Nixon promised the government agencies that they can have several thousand inspectors, if they need them, to stop fuel price gouging." The government truly enjoyed total immunity in the energy crises. It could devote full resources to creating fuel shortages, and in plain view of the national press corps it could boast of such efforts while simultaneously being characterized as the solution to the crises.

It should be noted, incidentally, that while Senate panels convened in the 1973–74 crisis to discuss whether the gas shortages were "real," the U.S. Federal Energy Office could have supplied a ready answer. The FEO *knew* the gas shortages were real because they were enforcing rules *purposely designed* to create them. *National Journal* reported in late 1973 that the Administration "is juggling energy policy in such a way as to funnel more of the available oil to industrial operations at the expense of car owners." The publication further reported that "In the jargon of the Federal Energy Office, this is known as 'maximizing the shortfall in gasoline.'[15]

If the camera crews were hungry for a story on who was contriving "to cut gasoline supplies as sharply as

---

[15]Richard Corrigan, "Energy Report/Federal Energy Office fuel priorities spell trouble for American motorists," in the *National Journal*, December 29, 1973, p. 1950.

practicable,"[16] it turns out that whole federal buildings in Washington were devoted to nothing more. Instead, the nightly news reports captured only the message that the authorities were sending out teams of federal agents to hunt down "price gougers." A scant 7% of the discussion of the crises' roots mentioned government allocation programs.

Thirty-five percent of the discussion on the origins of the crises dwelled on the oil industry as the prime perpetrator, Media Institute researchers found. Of these stories, 20% were given to industry denials, almost always presented by industry personnel who themselves were immediately discredited because of their perceived economic interest in the matter. The remaining 80% of the discussion of the domestic oil industry as the cause of the crises was devoted to finding hoaxes or oil company conspiracies (21% of this anti-industry discussion); 29% concerned excessive oil company profits, price gouging or withholding supplies; and 11% focused on the unreliability of industry data. The remaining 39% was a generic attack on the industry.

Taken collectively, the industry was portrayed not as a large cross-section of American society, nor a group of imperfect social organizations trying to make a living, nor an industry composed of thousands of intense rivals, but as an abstract model of cynical economic perfection. The petroleum industry, in the eyes of TV reporters, was not burdened with the mundane concerns of lesser businesses always nervous about remaining one step ahead, but was privileged to indulge its darkest desires to reap massive profits. And even more to the ideal of perfect economic evil was OPEC, a conglomeration so bizarre and fearful that its members could whimsically engage in "arbitrary pricing action," as Deputy Secretary

---

[16]IBID.

of Energy John O'Leary told CBS in December 1978.

This view was popular with the television press who reported that OPEC froze oil prices for three months "as a good-will gesture," as NBC termed it in March 1974. Nelson Benton of CBS questioned, in January 1979, "how long Saudi Arabia and other producers will pump more oil than normal to help fill the gap." And in March 1979 NBC's popular David Brinkley was led to denounce OPEC's price increases thusly: "Since all this bears no relation to the cost of production, or even to the needs of the producers, the only other reason must be greed or gouging."

In the second crisis, Senator Henry Jackson explained why he doubted the windfall profits tax would pass: "I've been fighting with the oil lobby, and I'm telling you, the word is greed."

Volume I

Chapter III

Whenever the price mechanism is prohibited from rationing scarce resources, non-price mechanisms will. Many who initially thought that getting rid of the former was a good idea soon came to reconsider when confronted with the reality of the latter. As Sowell describes it:

> One of the more dramatic recent examples of the effect of forcibly keeping prices below the market level has been the so-called "gasoline crisis" of 1979. Because of the complexities in long-standing government regulations controlling the price of gasoline, their full effect began to be felt in the Spring of 1979. As in the case of rent control, the effects were *not* primarily on the quantity of the physically defined product—gallons of gasoline in this case—but on the auxiliary services not articulated in the law. Just as rent control tends to reduce such auxiliary services as maintenance, heat, hot water, so controlling the price of gasoline reduced such auxiliary services as hours of service at filling stations, credit card acceptance, and checking under the hood. Indeed, what was called a "gasoline shortage" was *primarily* a shortage of hours of service at filling

stations, and the traumatic effects of this indicate that unarticulated aspects of the physically defined product are by no means incidental. In New York City, for example, the average filling station was open 110 hours a week in September 1978 and only 27 hours a week in June 1979. The actual amount of gasoline pumped declined by only a few percentage points, while the hours of service declined by 75 percent.[17]

Now the bitter truth is that when the government dared to lower retail gas prices, the shortages, disruptions and uncertainties that Sowell speaks of were so monumental and disturbing to the body politic that, after sufficient scolding of the "oil magnates," the retail controls were eased upward until they were no longer "binding." That is, if gas were selling for $1.25 a gallon, the controlled prices would be $1.45. Yet, the *crude* oil price controls remained. They were so stringent that when we were importing OPEC crude for nearly $40 a barrel in early 1980, the majority of our domestic label was priced at an average of under $11.[18] What a bargain that cheap U.S. crude must have been—*if* you could get your hands on it.[19]

Given the frenzied popularity of this below-market petrol, the demand exceeded the supply. Who got the cheap stuff? With the price mechanism quashed, a non-price means of rationing was called for—and the government allocation program was created. Controlled crude oil was "allocated" to refineries on the

---

[17]Sowell, pp. 181–182.

[18]Joseph P. Kalt, *The Economics and Politics of Oil Price Regulation: Federal Policy in the Post-Embargo Era* (Cambridge, MA: M.I.T. Press, 1981), pp. 18, 21.

[19]There were other policies (i.e. "entitlements") distinct from crude oil price controls (although not completely unrelated to them), which may have, in fact, marginally lowered pump prices by a few pennies per gallon. What is important to understand here, is that crude oil price controls did create a bargain-priced input for refiners which was *not* "passed along" to consumers in the form of lower gasoline prices.

basis of bureaucratic notions of equity, regulatory tinkering and ... political pull.

A group of "small" refineries (notoriously inefficient) lobbied Congress, and got a good tanker of it (13% of price-controlled oil in 1979).[20] The "small refinery bias" ended up wasting several billion dollars in excessive processing expenditures as small refineries blossomed overnight in the richly fertilized soil of subsidies, (not to mention the millions of gallons of gasoline which more efficient refineries could have recovered from the same crude).[21] Out of the gushers of Washington, D.C. spouted a new black gold called "entitlements."

Between 1974 and 1980, the "entitlements program", virtually unheard of outside the whispers of lobbyists, regulators, corporate attorneys and oil company executives, became a $14.5 billion a year tax and subsidy program benefitting certain companies *within* the oil industry.[22] It sprang from the "unfair" results of oil price controls, and worked something like this: Any company's "entitlement" *privilege* was another company's "entitlement" *obligation*. Companies with extensive domestic reserves under lock and key couldn't use their crude, but had to sell it to other companies lacking such reserves at the bargain basement tab. In other words, you could "own" American crude but you couldn't refine it. (What happened in practice, of course, was that companies did refine the oil they owned, but they had to pay *other* oil companies that were "entitled" to it for the thrill.) The stated purpose of the program was to "equalize the cost of crude" across all U.S. refiners; not only did the plan fail to do that, but its major domestic effects were: (1) to subsidize and thereby create costly, inefficient re-

---

[20]James B. Ramsey, *The Oil Muddle: Control vs. Competition* (Ethics and Public Policy Center: Washington, D.C., 1981), p. 80.
[21]IBID.
[22]Kalt, op. cit., p. 233.

fineries with political muscle; and (2) to encourage increased imports of high cost insecure foreign oil through the incredibly Byzantine entitlements shell game.[23]

All of this analysis was available to policy makers, and the television news medium, before the second oil crisis hit. A widely circulated Rand Corporation study, for instance, concluded in January 1977 that decontrol would *not* result in higher retail petroleum prices and that the only lasting effects of the regulatory scheme were to shuffle profits *within* the oil business.

In "Petroleum Regulation: The False Dilemma of Decontrol," economists Charles Phelps and Rod Smith noted what was common knowledge amongst those familiar with the data: "Existing analyses, with which we agree, conclude that the crude oil price ceilings most certainly reduce U.S. oil production and hence increase U.S. dependence on foreign sources." They found that removing *retail* price controls "would have no effect on product prices," and that removing *crude* oil price controls "would reduce dependence on foreign oil" without raising U.S. energy prices at the pump. "Thus the opportunities for decontrol," they wrote, "present a political challenge to the new (Carter) Administration. The choice is reduced dependence on foreign oil or continuation of the current

---

[23]A simple story about oil price regulations quickly ceases to be simple. It would be misleading to say that *all* importers of overseas oil, for instance the Aramco partners, were subsidized by entitlements. In general, entitlements helped domestic refiners and integrated oil companies which were relatively weak in domestic crude production and strong in refining. Figures from the years 1977, 1978 and 1979 illustrate the varying effects. Of the four U.S. partners in Aramco, Exxon and Texaco appear to have been hurt by entitlements in all three years, in that they were relatively high in the ratio of their U.S. crude production to refining. The other two firms, Mobil and Standard Oil of California, appear to have been subsidized by entitlements in each year, SOCAL quite substantially.

multi-billion dollar transfers within the industry."[24]

Until the advice was partially heeded, OPEC touched all the bases when it came to bat against U.S. energy policy. First we presented them with price controls on U.S. production, driving out domestic drilling and exploration activities which were competitive to Arab oil, and prompting an American shortfall that could only be filled in the international market. To compound the problem the entitlements program actually effected subsidies to U.S. firms for *importing* OPEC crude (in the form of privileges to refine so much cheap U.S. oil). This subsidy amounted to over 20% of the price of a barrel of international oil in the mid-1970s.[25]

The system of rewards and punishments was driving U.S. energy policy into such a perverse—and totally unnecessary—configuration that by April 1979 President Carter was forced to ask Congress for a gradual decontrol of crude oil prices, accompanied by a so-called Windfall Profits Tax (WPT) which, in actuality, is a sales tax collected at the derrick rather than at the gas pump (that is to say, the tax is *not* on profits, but on a percent of the sales price). On January 28, 1981 President Reagan speeded the oil decontrol timetable, removing all crude and (non-binding) retail price controls. As William Tucker announced in the December 1981 issue of *Harpers*: "With that simple act, the energy crisis of the 1970s has ended."[26]

The reaction to the surprise decontrol (which had been scheduled to arrive nine months later without Reagan's executive action) was quite revealing indeed. "Consumer groups" blasted the move as a payoff to

---

[24]Charles E. Phelps and Rodney T. Smith, "Petroleum Regulation: The False Dilemma of Decontrol" (Santa Monica: Rand Corporation, January 1977), pp. vi, viii.

[25]La Force, op. cit., p. 16.

[26]William Tucker, "The Energy Crisis is Over," *Harper's* Magazine, December 1981, p. 34.

the oil interests, and forecast phenomenal gas prices once the companies "could charge whatever they wanted." Prices did quickly rise 7–10 cents a gallon—but not from the removal of price controls *per se.* Given the fact that retail price controls were *above* the prices charged prior to decontrol, this point is self-evident. There was no legal prohibition against retailers charging more before. But, in that the entitlements program paid U.S. refiners to import more OPEC crude, this created a higher supply of refined oil and a slightly lower price. When price controls were removed, entitlements were abandoned automatically, because there was no longer any price-controlled oil to which anyone was entitled.

Oil imports have been dramatically reduced since oil decontrol was initiated in mid-1979. We now import less than 30% of our oil, down from over 50% at the height of the entitlements program in 1977–78. Domestic energy consumption has been markedly cut. The 7%–8% annual growth trend of the 1960s and 70s has been stood on its head; domestic consumption fell by 10% during 1980 and 1981, and was dropping at a 7% annual rate in the first months of 1982.[27] Part of this reduction in consumption, to be sure, was the result of the recession. But a very important component has been rational consumer response to price-induced conservation. The *Wall Street Journal* reported:

> In recent years, consumers in much of the world have invested billions of dollars in energy-conservation measures, and industries have made long-term moves away from oil to other, cheaper fuels. Experts, furthermore, see a weakening of the historical link between economic growth and energy

---

[27]Tor Meloe, Chief Economist of Texaco Inc., as quoted in "Latest Oil Uncertainty Concerns Drop in Price Rather than Big Rise," in *The Wall Street Journal,* March 8, 1982, p. 1 and p. 8.

use. Growth always had seemed to require a concomitant increase in energy consumption. In the past few years, however, the amount of energy, particularly from the crude oil, needed to produce a given degree of economic expansion has declined markedly.[28]

A complementary effect of crude oil price decontrol has been a rise in domestic energy production. U.S. oil exploration was the boom industry of the early 1980s, registering a 34% increase in 1980 and an additional 28% rise in the first half of 1981.[29] This broke a drilling record established in 1956 when domestic oil drilling became too expensive to compete with cheap overseas oil. And, perhaps of greatest shock value is the telling fact that, in the first nine months of decontrol, the inflation-adjusted profits of every one of the domestic "Seven Sisters" (the five U.S. corporations are Exxon, Mobil, Standard of California, Texaco and Gulf) *dropped*. So much for price controls protecting consumers from the greed of the corporate giants!

In the end, what we can and must say about federal energy policies is simply that they were a preposterous boondoggle. They did not deliver us "Project Independence," but had to be abandoned so that we might end the debilitating vulnerability to hostile foreign sources that they engendered. They did not lower gasoline prices, and soon after price controls were abolished, gas prices (between March 1981 and March 1982) fell by a dramatic 20.1% in real terms.[30] They

---

[28]Youssef M. Ibrahim and David Ignatius, "As Oil Use Declines, Experts See a Slowing in Price Increases," in *The Wall Street Journal*, January 27, 1982, p. 1.

[29]Union Oil Company letter to employees and stockholders, January 20, 1981.

[30]Computed from figures announced by Dan Lundberg, author of the "Lundberg Letter," as reported on ABC Radio network news, March 9, 1982; and most recent consumer price index available from the Department of Labor, Bureau of Labor Statistics: "CPI Detailed Report, February 1982."

did not punish OPEC; when controls went, the international price of crude plummeted. They did not punish the oil companies with political friends, but only those with drilling rigs on U.S. soil. All in all, our policies were penny stupid and pound foolish. Are we now in a position to understand the words of energy economist Walter Mead, a consultant to several federal agencies, in the July 22, 1977 issue of *Science* magazine:

> Professional economists who have specialized in energy economics almost to a man have argued for greater reliance on market forces and less government interference in energy problems. Their strong preference for market solutions is not because they are philosophical conservatives. Rather they are acutely aware of the poor record of government interference in the energy market. That record is one of massive and repeated resource misallocation.

Are the findings of the 1976 version of the President's Task Force on FEA regulations, headed by Yale Professor Paul MacAvoy, such a mystery?

> FEA regulations as they now exist confer few, if any benefits on the public.... In return for this lack of benefits and sense of false security, the American businessman, the taxpayer, and the petroleum consumer must incur higher costs than might otherwise be the case. Indeed continuation of the present regulatory mechanism will result in long-run inefficiencies for the American economy.[31]

Are we ready to understand the now-realized plea of Professor Lester Thurow, in his 1980 *Zero Sum Society*?

---

[31] Paul W. MacAvoy, editor, *Federal Energy Administration Regulation Report of the Presidential Task Force* (Washington, D.C.: American Enterprise Institute, 1977), p. 146.

One solution to the energy problem is simply to let the price of energy rise in accordance with that of imported oil. This would solve the problem in the sense that there would be no gas lines, no shortages, and no Energy Department full of complex and sometimes counterproductive regulations ... The regulatory approach ... suffers from a more fatal flaw than inconvenience. Government regulations can control prices and to a lesser extent production, but in our system they cannot control new investments. No one can be forced to invest. Eventually new investments are necessary, and they will not be made unless they are as profitable as investments made in countries that do not control energy prices. This leads to increasingly severe shortages, as the necessary new facilities are not built to accommodate rising demands and new products.... Eventually we are forced to decide whether we want free market pricing ... or a nationalized energy industry.[32]

---

[32]Lester Thurow, *The Zero-Sum Society* (New York: Basic Books, 1980), pp. 28–9, 33–4, 191.

The networks paid scant attention to the real debate, and in fact the central political and economic policy issue at stake: non-market solutions (rationing, regulation, price controls) versus market solutions (deregulation, decontrol). The networks generally presented the solution to the oil crises as a choice among non-market measures: conservation vs. rationing vs. forms of regulation and price controls.

Volume I

Chapter IV

When television news considered the harmful implications of price controls, the view presented was inevitably personalized and trivialized. So it was that the disincentives of price ceilings to producers were reported as the gimmickry of avaricious businessmen. Rather than investigate the veracity of the charge that oilmen would have an interest in creating a shortage, the "investigators" were ready to strike at any sign of "withholding supplies."

Consider stories discussing the crises' roots: 7% blame the government's allocation system, while only 3% accuse either other federal regulations or price controls. The hitch is that the allocation system was necessitated only by the existence of price controls set below market clearing levels. In the face of equilibrium market prices, gasoline is simply allocated to wherever consumers are willing to pay the going price. Reporters were unable to connect the source of the problem (price controls) with the allocation system. It could hardly be expected that, operating on such an information set, they would unleash new insights on the program itself.

But the most embarrassing breakdown was the

near-universal failure to discuss seriously any of the actions that would, in fact, come to *solve* the energy crises. The eventual three-fold solution included: 1) tremendous advances in energy efficiency (most notably: small car desirability) since prices shot above the dollar/gallon mark in early 1979; 2) a sudden reversal in declining U.S. oil production; and 3) an end to the "entitlements" subsidy for importing foreign oil. In stories discussing solutions, conservation was the most discussed means, but specifically *non-price* conservation. The intuition was that high prices really were irrelevant in stopping wasteful consumption, which was not the product of low prices but of wasteful habits. This called for made-in-Washington conservation of the kind feared by economist Robert J. Michaels, writing in the *Los Angeles Times* in 1979:

> The House of Representatives recently voted down legislation that would have required everyone to give up using his auto for one day a week. Something like it will come, sooner or later. Odd-even rules and weekend driving restrictions are the modern analog of Sunday closing laws. Civil libertarians aggressively fought these laws, which were supported by members of religious groups who claimed that the soul is too important to be left to the discretion of its owner. Today, we have people who make the same argument about carburetors.[33]

Rationing was the second most popular "solution" at 21%. On June 28, 1979, CBS' Richard Wagner, describing the "Oregon Plan" for odd/even gas rationing, put the choices clearly: " ... the Oregon experiment will doubtless be watched carefully by energy officials around the country to see if a strictly voluntary plan can work and thus make compulsory rationing of fuel a step the nation won't have to take."

---

[33]Robert J. Michaels, "Hell No, We Won't Go (to the Energy War)," *Los Angeles Times*, August 19, 1979, op-ed page.

Continued regulation and price controls were the third most frequently talked about solution. Decontrol and deregulation, which did in fact solve the energy crises, were mentioned in only one out of every twenty-five "solutions" discussion.

The networks' unwillingness to believe that economic forces were worth mentioning carried over into the reportage of OPEC. For some reason, OPEC was viewed as a *political* adversary much more than as a profit-maximizing economic agent. The international oil cartel was depicted as a hostile foreign force, assembled to punish the United States for political transgressions. This portrayal effectively served to diffuse questions concerning OPEC's interests in U.S. energy policy. When Congress extended price controls and entitlements at President Ford's request in late 1975, the bill became known amongst energy economists as "The OPEC Relief Act of 1975." Yet the television broadcast medium failed to see any such relationship. It was therefore quite elementary a task for U.S. politicians to pledge to extend domestic price controls to prevent U.S. oil companies from sharing the windfalls created by OPEC. It became a matter of common interest, of course: OPEC didn't want American crude oil producers to share their windfalls, either. Both the politicians and the Arab oil interests prevailed, until decontrol.[34]

The news void on the *effects* of the government's regulatory pattern emerges as the blank check upon which ten years of anti-energy programs were written. When crude oil price controls came up, no one

___

[34]The Arabs continue to be taken care of, to a great extent, by the Windfall Profits Tax. This levy can only be applied to homegrown crude, thus making OPEC oil more highly demanded than it would be in the absence of the tax. The tax, therefore, carries over some of the distortive effects of U.S. energy regulation; but the simple removal of price controls has both erased the grossest subsidies to OPEC (in that "entitlements" are gone because there is no more price-controlled crude to be entitled to) and the possibility of retail gasoline shortages. (For a critique of the misallocative effects of the WPT, see Kalt, supra Note 18.)

thought to ask if retail gas prices were actually being lowered by such controls. President Nixon's much-heralded "Project Independence" was taken at face value as a scheme to reduce imports, and when imports skyrocketed under his program it still managed to escape news scrutiny.

The plain truth was that price controls on *crude* were not lowering the price of *retail* gasoline, which is quite a different product, but the empirical question as to what would happen to gasoline pump prices after decontrol was nonetheless taken as axiomatic. Leslie Stahl, reporting for CBS News on April 26, 1979 referred to problems "after prices start their inexorable climb because of decontrol"; Rod Mac-Leish's CBS Commentary of April 7, 1979 had warned of public outrage "once decontrolled oil prices rocket upwards"; Mike Jensen, on the NBC broadcast of December 18, 1978 was heard stating flatly that price decontrol "would raise the price of all petroleum products here another seven or eight cents a gallon, although it probably would be spread out over many months."

What the networks didn't know was that *crude* oil price controls, an enormously important policy upon which they had reported for better than half a decade, had failed to shield American consumers from paying the world price of refined gasoline. The economics as to why the controls worked or didn't work is straight-forward. The underlying reality, however, is that this question, which turns out to be so fundamental to the whole crisis, was ignored by television news. It has only been revived thanks to the "phenomenal" (in light of popular analysis) decline in oil prices post-decontrol.

Instead, the shortage was blamed on "wasteful American consumers" and the vulgar inefficiencies of the middle-class lifestyle. Legal action to enforce lower thermostat settings, slower highway speeds, darker homes, fewer airline flights and more carpooling were discussed, in aggregate more than twice as often as energy price decontrol—which would create all of the above conservation measures and countless more. When non-price conservation and/or rationing were advanced in 50% of all stories dealing with possible solutions (as The Media Institute's study found) where was the enterprising journalist to dig up the scoop revealing even one instance where these platitudes had been forged into successful public policy? Instead, viewers were treated to a news medium preoccupied with motives, moralisms and pieties; a tacit censorship of any considered examination of policy effects, of price effects. And how were the imminently important conflicts of interest among OPEC, U.S. oil refiners, U.S. oil importers, U.S. crude oil producers, and other U.S. industries presented by television news reporters? There is little evidence that reporters were even aware of them.

Despite ample time for reporters to study in preparation for the 1978–79 crisis, television news coverage of the actual effects of the controls (distinct from bromides championing the "public interest" or "Project Independence") was nonexistent. When criticism came to rest on government regulations, it was inevitably reported either as a matter of insufficient government involvement, or as a critique launched by obviously self-interested oil executives. Of course, the U.S. oil industry has never in its history been unified behind a policy of free market competition in energy, and during the 1970s was continually supporting various means of protectionism. But not even the most blatant industry nonsense was impeached, for instance, the fact that the control regimen was a massive *windfall* to refiners as it suppressed the price they paid and propped up the price they got. In the first year of decontrol, 1981, refineries had their worst financial year in recent history.[35]

It was apparently thought useless to apply rigorous standards to the accuracy of industry statements when the underlying theme—that oil companies wanted to fleece the American public—was appropriately served by making the oil industry the source of all arguments for decontrol.[36] This tactic amounted to a guilt-by-association technique which was relaxed only when President Carter tied price decontrol to the enormous tax increase known as the Windfall Profits Tax. This program will last until the early 1990s, and bring an estimated $227.3 billion into federal coffers, collecting "roughly $.70 of every $1.00 of crude oil price increase."[37] What completely escaped notice were the self-interests of business in supporting a continued regimen of controls—always with the proper "reforms." How the most flagrant appeals sneaked through is difficult to explain. In April 1977 the then president of ARCO, Thornton Bradshaw, was cited in *Time* Magazine enunciating his view on decontrol. "The signals provided by the free enterprise system must be supplemented by government signals," he contended. "Government must set the goals as well as the incentives and disincentives." Unknowingly, *Time* then blew his audacious cover by reporting that "Bradshaw would even accept Government price-setting—but only on one product, crude oil ... "[38] Not so incidentally ARCO is both a net demander of crude

---

[35]"Oil Refineries Shutting Down at Rapid Pace," *Los Angeles Times*, January 11, 1982, p. 1.

[36]The supposition that oil companies were out to fleece the public was true enough, of course, and a good many oil firms did just this through the federal regulatory system. This point went right past the television reporting. Market competition, free entry and product rivalry are the forces that economists have found most dependably effective in channeling this base, but incessant, desire toward positive satisfaction of consumer welfare.

[37]Kalt, op. cit., p. 22.

[38]"Opening the Debate," *Time* Magazine, April 25, 1977.

(meaning it buys more crude than it sells) and a large retailer.

Why was so little time devoted to examining those who stood to gain so much? One cannot help but be drawn to the over ripe conclusion that the media's "investigators" were seduced by a romantic plot and that when that story line crashed into reality, it was the latter that cracked and crumbled. Businessmen such as Thornton Bradshaw, who espoused their economic interests in favor of (profit-creating) regulation, were even held up as noble-minded futurists when compared to competing oil industry low-lifes who, if they were in the employ of crude oil producers, would champion the (profit-creating) decontrol solution. Moreover, the universally observable ramifications of simple price theory—the automatic responses of consumer demand and producer supply to changes in price—were either ignored or castigated. This presumably served to shore up a generally held world view confirming catastrophe.

History has not been kind to such views. In 1977, Carter energy chief James Schlesinger argued for his Administration's regulatory game plan by noting that, "We have a classic Malthusian case of exponential growth against a finite resource."[39] *Time* Magazine nodded: "The U.S. will exhaust its oil and natural gas resources within the next 30 or 40 years."[40] In his 1980 best-seller *Paper Money*, popular financial scribe "Adam Smith" explained it another way: "There is not a single expert who expects (American production) to rise."[41] And the price? "The price," he proffered, "will go not only where economic demand takes it, for the reality of the world is more ragged than the world of economists. The price will go where OPEC takes it, and that price is determined not only by economic

---

[39]IBID.
[40]IBID.
[41]Adam Smith, op. cit., p. 216.

demand but by political opportunity. The present secretary-general of OPEC says he has looked over the numbers, and he thinks maybe $60 a barrel would be fair, and, like the economists', his guess is as good as anybody's."[42]

It appears today that the world of reality (and the world post-price controls) is a little more ragged than the world of Mr. "Smith." His book, which bears a 1980 copyright, was made obsolete before it made it into paperback. After a decade of dramatically declining U.S. oil production, which he notes, "Smith" gives forecasts of accelerated future declines. The 1980 trend line was obliterated by 1981's trends. The decline was stopped and oil and gas drilling skyrocketed. One salubrious result is that, due to the gradual relaxation of restrictive ceiling prices on new natural gas finds, an increasing percentage of our energy is being provided by this non-polluting fossil fuel. Current estimates are that U.S. oil output will be the same in 1985 as it was in 1979; "Smith" gave us a 12½% drop. And the only reason we do not see rapid increases in petroleum output is because price-induced conservation has made the American economy so much more fuel efficient that the quantity demanded is falling precipitously; if continued high quantities were demanded, and the price were to ooze up to "Smith's" $60/barrel, petroleum production would gush forth like a Gulf of Mexico oil spill.

In embarrassing fashion, it was only when the Carter Administration began its drive for deregulation in June 1979 that the television news medium, again taking its governmental cue, began discussing the relevant policy measures that lifted us out of the abyss. Far more stories in the second crisis, consequently, dealt with the problem of government controls and possible gains from eliminating them. But

---

[42]IBID., p. 203.

when President Carter threw in the regulatory towel and asked Congress to (gradually) decontrol oil and natural gas in April 1979, CBS commentator Rod MacLeish embraced the President's plan but refused to change tunes: "The Carter plan for decontrolling domestic oil prices," said MacLeish, "is a final shot in the head to the chief premise that this country has operated on since the first Rockefeller (sic) drilled the first oil well in Titusville, Pennsylvania. Decontrols will afflict the public with higher oil prices."[43]

The price of this policy was steep because the higher prices anticipated from decontrol would induce higher oil company profits as well. The fear of this political horror, which had haunted the Nixon Administration and had prevented *it* from considering oil price decontrol at the crisis' outset[44], resulted in near universal concern over the hopelessness of passing the Windfall Profits Tax. "A tax on windfall profits is regarded by the critics as ridiculous because the oil lobby and the President's other opponents won't let Congress pass it," announced MacLeish. On April 23, 1979 Ray Brady reported, "if the oil companies don't want a windfall profits tax, said one senator, there won't be a tax." And by April 25, Senator Edward Kennedy was moved to exclaim on the CBS Evening News with Walter Cronkite: "Well, Mr. Schlesinger, you're about the only one in Washington, I dare say in the country, who believes that you're going to get a realistic windfall profits tax."

The Administration got a Windfall Profits Tax which will raise over $200 billion through the 1980s,

---

[43]John D. Rockefeller, Sr. was but a teen-ager in Cleveland when the first oil was drilled in Titusville, Pennsylvania. At any rate, he was later to go into the *refining* business.

[44]"Congress fails to pass emergency energy bill; House, Senate act on reorganization proposals," in the *National Journal*, December 29, 1973, p. 1953. "The Nixon Administration Dec. 19 relaxed price controls on domestic crude oil and urged Congress to impose a 'windfall profits' tax on oil producers until world supply catches up with demand."

and which was identified by many as the largest single tax increase in U.S. history. But once they started believing the rhetoric and marveling at this perfect model of monopolistic exploitation called "Big Oil", it was hard to stop. And for so simple, natural and bipartisan a political issue as the Windfalls Profits Tax— originally proposed by President Richard M. Nixon in the very first weeks of the 1973–74 crisis.[45]

---

[45]"Energy Report/President forms federal energy body with broad regulation, price control powers," in the *National Journal*, December 8, 1973, p. 1831. "It would take a large price increase to bring about the kind of consumption reduction (Federal Energy Administration chief) Simon is looking for ... But a large increase in the price of gasoline likely would result in much higher oil company profits, an eventuality which both the Administration and the oil companies view as an unacceptable political liability."

One need not have a political or economic point of view to recognize the imbalance and asymmetry in the use of government and non-government sources, and the imbalance in the presentation of causes and solutions.

Volume I

Conclusion

At bottom, network television news coverage of the oil crises failed to grasp the story being covered, and to challenge those in both the public and private sectors who manipulated energy policy to the detriment of the common weal. How could this happen in so sophisticated a medium, in such advanced an age? Perhaps it is a matter of methodology, of a peculiar approach to social problems that precludes the bulk of available empirical evidence, and boxes the researcher into a narrow and blinding corner.

In one of the most thought provoking arguments concerning the differing methods for viewing society, Thomas Sowell has contrasted "intellectuals," who are interpreted to include the journalism profession, with other participants in society. Sowell finds a fundamental antagonism between intellectuals, who "tend to conceive of accountability solely in terms of their own processes of articulated rationality," and other social elites, such as business executives, who survive by satisfying "the market" in some *un*articulated—but no less important—sense. The lifeblood of the practicing academic, for example, is the "model," an abstract framework whereby he may chart the interaction of all relevant variables on their way to a rationally planned, or at least rationally understood, conclusion. News reporters, similarly, must take even greater care to follow carefully the purposeful behavior of the particular people who actually get up and make something happen, because it is pretty tough to catch "social forces" on videotape. It does not leave Sowell astonished that these articulators of human processes should have trouble identifying with those for whom life is not so easy to paint. "A businessman whose whole economic future is staked on the correctness of his assessments of consumer desires or technological possibilities is regarded by intellectuals as unaccountable, because he does not articulate to anyone." But Sowell notes a dangerous asymmetry: "Conversely, psychiatrists, psychologists and social workers whose articulated assessments lead to dangerous criminals being turned loose are *not* accused of being unaccountable, even though they suffer no penalties for the robberies, assaults, or murders committed by those released—not even the embarrassment of having a personal box score kept on the criminals released on their recommendations."[46]

The narrowness of vision that obscures "unarticulated" market forces from view, blocked by a gaudy vision of White Hats and Black Hats—human emotions we can taste, touch and feel—the planners and the profligate, the wise and the wasteful, the victims and the exploiters, is really not so very advanced, or intellectual, after all. Indeed, it is in the interests of *accountability* that this paper raises such questions in the national debate over the quality of America's television news.

The ebb and flow of spontaneous social forces are just not as provocative as the titillating characters who, as "Big Oil" or OPEC, or Wasteful American Gas Guz-

---

[46]Sowell, op. cit., p. 364.